C O N T E N T S

W9-AXN-466

Introduction 5
How to Use This Resource 6

1. **Baptism in Water** 7
   1. *An elementary principle: Doctrine of baptisms* 8
   2. *Baptism in water is a demonstration of obedience* 8
   3. *Baptism in water makes a public announcement* 10
   4. *Baptism in water shows we are dead to sin and alive to Christ* ... 11
   5. *Baptism in water illustrates a New Testament circumcision* 12
   6. *Baptism in water shows we are obeying God* 13
   7. *Be baptized in water!* 14
      Teaching Outline 44

2. **More Baptisms** 17
   1. *Baptism into the body of Christ* 18
   2. *God's wonderful family* 18
   3. *Baptism of fire* 19
   4. *Drinking the cup* 21
   5. *Count it all joy* 21
   6. *Persevering in our trials* 22
   7. *On fire for Jesus* 23
      Teaching Outline 46

3. **Baptism in the Holy Spirit-Part 1** 25
   1. *The promise of the Holy Spirit* 26
   2. *The Holy Spirit lives within every believer* 27
   3. *You shall receive power!* 28
   4. *We receive by faith* 29
   5. *Want to be effective? It's your decision* 30
   6. *Saul's second experience with the Holy Spirit* 31
   7. *Experiencing His power for yourself* 32
      Teaching Outline 48

4. **Baptism in the Holy Spirit-Part 2** 35
   1. *Receive God's good gift* 36
   2. *What about tongues?* 37
   3. *I wish you all spoke in tongues* 38
   4. *Bypassing the devil!* 39
   5. *Kinds of tongues* 40
   6. *Eagerly desire* 42
   7. *Continue to be filled with the Spirit* 43
      Teaching Outline 50

Journaling space for reflection questions.................... 52
Extra devotional questions 60

Books in this Series

This is the third book in a twelve-book series designed to help believers to build a solid biblical foundation in their lives.

1 **Knowing Jesus Christ as Lord**
   God's purpose for our lives through a personal relationship with Jesus

2 **The New Way of Living**
   True repentance and faith toward God

3 **New Testament Baptisms**
   Four baptisms including baptism in water and baptism in the Holy Spirit

4 **Building For Eternity**
   The hope of the resurrection, the laying on of hands and eternal judgment

5 **Living in the Grace of God**
   Applying God's grace to everyday living

6 **Freedom from the Curse**
   Christ brings freedom to every area of our lives

7 **Learning to Fellowship with God**
   How to deepen our relationship with Jesus Christ

8 **What is the Church?**
   Finding our place in God's family

9 **Authority and Accountability**
   How to respond to leadership and fellow believers God places in our lives

10 **God's Perspective on Finances**
   How God wants His people to handle money

11 **Called to Minister**
   Every Christian's call to serve

12 **The Great Commission**
   Our purpose for living on this planet

A corresponding *Biblical Foundations for Children* book is also available (see page 63).

Introduction

The foundation of the Christian faith is built on Jesus Christ and His Word to us, the Holy Bible. This twelve-book *Biblical Foundation Series* includes elementary principles every Christian needs to help lay a strong spiritual foundation in his or her life. In this third Biblical Foundation book, *New Testament Baptisms,* we look at another of the six foundational doctrines of the Christian faith found in Hebrews 6:1-2—**the doctrine of baptisms:** *Therefore, leaving the discussion of the elementary principles of Christ, let us go on to perfection, not laying again the foundation of repentance from dead works and of faith toward God, of the doctrine of baptisms, of laying on of hands, of resurrection of the dead, and of eternal judgment (NKJ).* This book covers four baptisms, including baptism in water (a sign of cleansing and remission of sin), baptism into the body of Christ (the Holy Spirit supernaturally places us into the "body" or "the family of God"), baptism of fire (facing suffering in our lives and persevering), and the baptism in the Holy Spirit (a new dimension of the Holy Spirit's power).

In this book, the foundation truths from the Word of God are presented with modern day parables that help you easily understand the basics of Christianity. Use this book and the other 11 *Biblical Foundation* books to lay a solid spiritual foundation in your life, or if you are already a mature Christian, these books are great tools to assist you in discipling others. May His Word become life to you today.

God bless you!

Larry Kreider

How to Use This Resource

Personal study

Read from start to finish as an individual study program to build a firm Christian foundation and develop spiritual maturity.

- Each chapter has a key verse excellent to commit to memory.
- Additional scriptures in gray boxes are used for further study.
- Each reading includes questions for personal reflection and room to journal at the end of the book.

Daily devotional

Use as a devotional for a daily study of God's Word.

- Each chapter is divided into 7-day sections for weekly use.
- Additional days at the end of the book bring the total number of devotionals to one complete month. The complete set of 12 books gives one year's worth of daily devotionals.
- Additional scriptures are used for further study.
- Each day includes reflection questions and a place to write answers at the end of the book.

Mentoring relationship

Use for a spiritual parenting relationship to study, pray and discuss life applications together.

- A spiritual father or mother can easily take a spiritual son or daughter through these Bible study lessons and use the reflection questions to provoke dialogue about what is learned.
- Read each day or an entire chapter at a time.

Small group study

Study this important biblical foundation in a small group setting.

- The teacher studies the material in the chapters and teaches, using the user-friendly outline provided at the end of the book.

Taught as a biblical foundation course

These teachings can be taught by a pastor or other Christian leader as a basic biblical foundation course.

- Students read an assigned portion of the material.
- In the class, the leader teaches the assigned material using the chapter outlines at the end of the book.

CHAPTER 1

Baptism in Water

KEY MEMORY VERSE

We were therefore buried with him through baptism into death in order that, just as Christ was raised from the dead through the glory of the Father, we too may live a new life.

Romans 6:4

An elementary principle:
Doctrine of baptisms

Being baptized is one of the first steps a new Christian should make. Baptism is an essential part of the spiritual foundation of a new Christian's life. When we think of baptism, we normally think of water baptism and its various modes—sprinkling, pouring, immersion. But there really are more kinds of baptisms mentioned in God's Word than water baptism. Let's look at Hebrews 6.

In addition to the previous foundational principles we learned in Biblical Foundation 2, (*repentance from dead works* and *faith toward God*), Hebrews, chapter 6, lists yet another elementary principle—the doctrine of baptisms. *Therefore, leaving the discussion of the elementary principles of Christ, let us go on to perfection, not laying again the foundation of...the doctrine of baptisms...(Hebrews 6:2 NKJ).*

Since this spiritual foundation is listed as plural—baptisms—it indicates that the Christian faith includes more than one kind of baptism. As we read through the New Testament, we discover there are four distinct types of baptisms: baptism in water, baptism into the body of Christ, baptism of fire, and baptism in the Holy Spirit. In this book, we will take a look at all four, starting with the Christian baptism in water.

REFLECTION
Name the four types of baptisms mentioned in the Bible. Think about how many of the four you have experienced.

Baptism in water is a demonstration of obedience

Water baptism, sometimes called *believer's baptism*, is for the purpose of identifying with Jesus. In the New Testament, once a person believed in Jesus for salvation, he was then baptized in water. Baptism is a sign of cleansing and forgiveness of sin—an act of faith and obedience. Jesus, Himself, introduces us to water baptism when He was baptized by John the Baptist.

John had been preaching a baptism of repentance for the forgiveness of sins (Mark 1:4). When people repented of their sins, they were water-baptized as the outward evidence that they had repented. Since it was an outward sign, it did not magically save them. The power in baptism was in the power of God, not in the water or the act itself.

"Then why," you may ask, "was Jesus baptized"? Jesus was without sin (1 Peter 2:21-22); He did not need to show evidence of confessing and repenting of sin. John pondered the same question when Jesus came to him to be baptized. Jesus gave John the answer to his question when he said, "Let it be so now; it is proper for us to do this to fulfill all righteousness" (Matthew 3:15).

Jesus was setting an example for Christian believers to follow— not simply as evidence that they had confessed and repented of their sins, but "to fulfill [complete] all righteousness." Christian baptism is an outward act of obedience by which the believer fulfills the inward righteousness he already has through faith in Christ's death and resurrection.

Jesus said that everywhere the gospel is preached, individuals will be saved when they believe. Baptism naturally followed. *Whoever believes and is baptized will be saved...(Mark 16:16).*

The natural succession and pattern of believing first and then being baptized is followed throughout the New Testament. Sometimes people ask, "I was baptized as an infant. Is infant baptism in the Bible?" Infant baptism is not mentioned in the Bible. The record of baptisms in the New Testament are of adults who were previously unbelievers. These believers were baptized after their belief and faith in Jesus. Since infants are incapable of exercising faith, and baptism is the outward sign of faith, it stands to reason that an infant is not eligible for baptism. Although there is not necessarily anything wrong with baptizing a baby as a form of dedication to the Lord, according to scripture, they should be baptized after they believe as an outward sign of faith.

REFLECTION
If you have been water baptized, recall your experience.

The key question to ask is this: Have you been baptized since you've believed? The Bible teaches us to be baptized in water after we believe in Jesus. It is a sign of our faith.

Baptism in water makes a public announcement

As a sign of our faith in Jesus, water baptism makes several bold statements. Let's look at these statements in the next four sections. First of all, the Bible tells us that water baptism is a public announcement of our decision to turn our backs on sin and live for Jesus Christ...*all should be baptized as a public announcement of their decision to turn their backs on sin (Mark 1:4 TLB).*

Baptism is a public announcement that we have taken a clear stand for Jesus Christ. In the early church, it was taken for granted that when someone turned his life over to Jesus Christ, his first step of obedience was water baptism...*Repent and be baptized, every one of you, in the name of Jesus Christ for the forgiveness of your sins...(Acts 2:38).*

When I was a youth worker, there were times when dozens of young people gave their lives to Jesus during a given week. We often baptized them the same day they were born again. Some were baptized in swimming pools, others in rivers and ponds, and still others in bathtubs. These water baptisms were very meaningful, spiritual times. Baptisms can take place in varied settings, large or small. Some baptisms can be planned ahead and attended by friends and family so they can be a part of the celebration.

No matter what method or in what setting, new Christians are making a public statement by participating in the physical, outward sign of their salvation by being baptized. This act of faith is a decision that empowers Christians to fulfill the Great Commission to wholeheartedly make and baptize disciples. *Therefore go and make disciples of all nations, baptizing them in the name of the Father and of the Son and of the Holy Spirit,*

REFLECTION
If you have been water-baptized, what does it mean to you, to Jesus, to your friends?

and teaching them to obey everything I have commanded you. And surely I am with you always, to the very end of the age (Matthew 28:19-20).

Baptism in water shows we are dead to sin and alive to Christ

A second reason why water baptism is so important is that it shows we are dead to sin and alive to Christ, according to Romans 6:4. *We were therefore buried with him through baptism into death in order that, just as Christ was raised from the dead through the glory of the Father, we too may live a new life.*

Water baptism is a sign of being buried to sin and resurrected to new life. Jesus was buried and resurrected two thousand years ago. We are buried with Him by baptism in a spiritual sense. We must be dead to ourselves before we can have new life. When we come to the cross, we die to our old way of living so that we can have the new resurrected life that God has promised.

When you go to a funeral and see a dead man, you know that he cannot respond to anything. He cannot be hurt physically or emotionally. He cannot feel pain. He is dead! When we are buried in Christ, our old nature no longer can do its own thing; it is dead. So then, spiritually speaking, our old life is dead.

Here's an example: Joe was a former gangster with the Mafia, who gave his life to Jesus. His life was permanently changed. A few weeks after he gave his life to the Lord, one of his Mafia brothers called him on the phone and said, "Hey, is Joe there?"

Joe answered, "No, Joe died," and hung up the phone. The truth is, Joe *had* died. He was a brand new Joe and was living a brand new life. The old Joe was dead, a new Joe had come, and Jesus Christ now lived in him. Water baptism is a sign that we have died to self and, with the power of God's glory, now walk in a new life.

Sometimes people ask, "How should a person be baptized?" The Greek word for *baptize* is *baptiso*, which means *to immerse*. We encourage people to be immersed in the water. Going into

REFLECTION
What is the spiritual explanation of going under and coming back up out of the water? Can you truly say that your "old self" is dead?

the watery grave of baptism is symbolic of dying to self, being buried and then resurrected as we come up out of the water.

You have been crucified with Christ. Your old "man" (evil nature) is dead. Through water baptism, you become dead to sin and alive to Christ.

Baptism in water illustrates a New Testament circumcision

This brings us to a third statement that water baptism makes. Water baptism is a type of New Testament circumcision. In the Old Testament circumcision, when an infant boy was eight days old, his foreskin was cut away as a sign of God's covenant to His people. It was a sign of faith just as it is in the New Testament. Colossians 2:11-12 says that submitting to the watery grave of baptism, just like circumcision, shows that our old sin nature has been cut away, supernaturally. *In him you were also circumcised, in the putting off of the sinful nature, not with a circumcision done by the hands of men but with the circumcision done by Christ, having been buried with him in baptism and raised with him through your faith in the power of God, who raised him from the dead.*

New Testament circumcision
Romans 2:29

The power of the sin nature that is inside you and me—that old nature that says, "I want to do what I want to do"—is symbolically cut away when we're baptized in water. It's a New Testament circumcision.

I once read about a man who had a very mean landlord who was always causing problems. One day, the landlord sold the property to a new landlord, a wonderful man. Sometime later, the first landlord came back and demanded that the tenant pay him. The tenant said, "What do you mean? You don't own this anymore. Go talk to my new landlord." When your old landlord, the devil, comes and tries to tell you that you are still under bondage to the old habits of the past—lying, criticism, lust, hatred, anger, or whatever—you can tell the devil you have a new landlord. His name is Jesus. Tell the devil, "Go talk to Jesus!"

When we are baptized in water, we are making a statement that the bondage of the past is broken. It's a supernatural work of God. Moses and the children of Israel were in bondage to the Egyptians, but when they came through the Red Sea, God's people were baptized and set free after coming through the water. *For I do not want you to be ignorant of the fact, brothers, that our forefathers were all under the cloud and that they all passed through the sea. They were all baptized into Moses in the cloud and in the sea (1 Corinthians 10:1-2).*

Having trusted God, by faith in Jesus, for freedom from the bondage of our past, we are then baptized. We don't always feel that we are freed from bondage. That's why it's important that we know it by faith. We live by the truth of His Word, not by our emotions. I remember flying into my hometown of Lancaster, Pennsylvania, one time and feeling sure we were going the wrong way. But we came into the right airport. The pilots were flying by the navigation equipment—and it was right. We should live our lives, not by every whim of our emotions, but according to God's navigation instrument, the Bible, which gives us the will of God.

Romans 6:14 says, *For sin shall not be your master....* Instead of seeing this scripture as a law, see it as a promise. God says that sin shall not have power over me because I am buried with Him in baptism. The old me is dead. I am a brand new person!

Our old, evil nature is rendered inoperative and through water baptism, we experience New Testament circumcision. Romans 6:6 states, *For we know that our old self was crucified with him so that the body of sin might be done away with, that we should no longer be slaves to sin.*

REFLECTION
As we pass through the water, we are symbolizing our freedom from our past bondage to Sin
(fill in the blank).
Why is it important not to rely on our feelings? my heart is a wicked deceitful thing.

The old has been cut away! We are living a new life with Jesus Christ inside of us.

Baptism in water shows we are obeying God

A fourth statement water baptism makes is that it shows we are obeying God. The Word of God instructs us to be baptized in water. We are exhorted to "believe and be baptized" (Mark 16:16). Water baptism symbolizes a spiritual cleansing, according to 1 Peter 3:21. *And this water symbolizes baptism that now saves you also—not the removal of dirt from the body but the pledge of a good conscience toward God. It saves you by the resurrection of Jesus Christ.*

It is the cleansing of the heart, not the outward ceremony that saves. Washing with water does little more than removing dirt. But being baptized shows that we are living with a clear conscience. We have an unwavering confidence in Jesus Christ. We are obeying the

Lord in all that He has asked us to do, and it brings a tremendous freedom into our lives.

Sometimes people ask, "What about a deathbed conversion? If someone gives his heart to Jesus and dies two minutes later and there is no time to baptize him, where does he spend eternity?" Remember, baptism does not save us. The blood of Jesus Christ saves us. Baptism is simply an act of obedience. After his profession of faith, the thief on the cross could not be water-baptized but Jesus said He would see him in paradise (Luke 23:40-43).

REFLECTION
What brings a clear conscience toward God?

Cleansing of the heart.

According to the examples given in the scriptures, and if we have the opportunity, we should be baptized as soon after conversion as possible. When Paul was in jail, the Philippian jailer gave his heart to Jesus. The jailer's whole household was baptized that night with water (Acts 16:33). While Philip was walking down a road one day, he met an Ethiopian official sitting in his chariot and reading the scriptures. Philip explained the good news about Jesus to him, and he was baptized as soon as they found some water (Acts 8:38). Crispus and his household, and many other Corinthians (Acts 18:8), believed and were baptized immediately.

Every believer, even a young child who has faith to be baptized should be encouraged to be baptized...*According to your faith, let it be to you (Matthew 9:29 NKJ)*. It should be noted, however, that a child should never be pressured into water baptism; he or she must desire it and be ready for it.

Be baptized in water!

If you have never been baptized in water, what are you waiting for? Do it today! We mentioned in Day 6 that when Jesus hung on the cross between two thieves, one of them was saved but there was no opportunity for him to come down from the cross and be baptized.

However, you and I have that opportunity. Although baptism does not save us, let's be obedient to the Word of God and take the opportunity to show we are dead to sin and alive to Christ. If you have any doubts about your baptism in water, I encourage you to be rebaptized. Doubts can cloud your faith and cast a shadow of condemnation on your life. Romans 14:23 says that...*everything that does not come from faith is sin.*

It's important that you are living and walking in faith. If you're not sure, be baptized in water so that you can be certain and the enemy cannot sow seeds of doubts in your mind. Water baptism is a physical act which reminds you of your faith and freedom in Jesus. You can point to it if the devil tries to lie to you and put doubt in your heart. You can say with assurance, "I was baptized in water and I know that I'm free. The old man, the former sinful nature, is cut off and has no power. Jesus Christ lives strong in my life." Talk to a pastor or small group leader to arrange for your water baptism.

I believe any believer in Christ can baptize another believer in water. You do not have to necessarily be a pastor or elder to perform a baptism. Paul, the apostle, often left water baptism to other believers in the church. He did it simply because they could help out this way. Paul knew his primary calling was to preach the gospel and to train others. *I am thankful that I did not baptize any of you except Crispus and Gaius...For Christ did not send me to baptize, but to preach the gospel...(1 Corinthians 1:14,17).*

REFLECTION
If you have doubts about your conversion and baptism, what can you do about it?

To summarize, water baptism is a sign of an inner cleansing of the heart. It is a public declaration that I have turned from sin to serve Jesus Christ as Lord. It shows that I am dead to sin and alive to Christ. It is a type of New Testament circumcision where the power of my old nature has been cut off. And most important of all, baptism in water is important because the Lord, in His Word, commands me to be baptized, and I want to be obedient to Him.

CHAPTER 2

More Baptisms

KEY MEMORY VERSE

...But one more powerful than I will come...
He will baptize you with the
Holy Spirit and with fire.
Luke 3:16

Baptism into the body of Christ

Baptism into the body of Christ is another kind of baptism mentioned in the New Testament. We learned earlier that the word *baptize* literally means *to put into*. When we're baptized in water, someone places us into the water. When we're baptized into the body of Christ, the Holy Spirit supernaturally places us into the "body" or "the family of God." *For we were all baptized by one Spirit into one body—whether Jews or Greeks, slave or free—and we were all given the one Spirit to drink (1 Corinthians 12:13).*

We are united by one Spirit as members of the body of Christ. God gives us other people in the body of Christ for support and encouragement. As we learn from each other, and get to know Jesus better, we are made complete by His Spirit. Jesus is the head of the body, and each believer makes up a part of His spiritual body on earth. We are here on earth to become Christ's hands, feet and tongue and other parts of the body with various functions, abilities and callings.

When a young man is newly married, he leaves his old family and is placed into a new family. As a new husband, he and his wife start a new unit of their own. Likewise, a new believer is supernaturally placed in

REFLECTION
Who baptizes you into the body of Christ?
Holy Spirit

the new family of God to begin life anew. Being baptized into the body of Christ is a supernatural work of God. We are placed, spiritually, into the body of Christ the moment we receive Jesus Christ as Lord. Because we belong to Christ, we are members and belong to each other.

God's wonderful family

When you are born again into God's family, you become a brother or sister in Christ to every other believer in the world. Being a part of the Lord's family is a wonderful blessing. You can meet a Christian brother or sister for the very first time from another nation and it seems like you have known them forever. You are a part of the same family!

Years ago, I visited the largest church in the world in Seoul, Korea. It was a beautiful experience meeting dozens of Korean believers, and although we did not speak the same language, we were able to sense that we were a part of the same spiritual family.

When John, the apostle, saw the throne of heaven in Revelation 5:9, he saw "living creatures and elders" (representing followers of Christ or the church in all nations and among all kinds of people), giving honor to Jesus. *And they sang a new song: "You are worthy to take the scroll and to open its seals, because you were slain, and with your blood you purchased men for God from every tribe and language and people and nation."*

God's wonderful family is made up of people from every nationality, race, and culture. We are all brothers and sisters through faith in our Lord Jesus Christ!

The Lord's family is awesome. Each of us has been born again by the Spirit of God. We are sons and daughters of the King of the uni- *burden 4the nations* verse, according to 2 Corinthians 6:18. *"I will be a Father to you, and you will be my sons and daughters," says the Lord Almighty.*

REFLECTION
Think about a time you experienced kinship with a believer from a different culture. What did you have in common?

Baptism of fire

DAY 3

Yet another kind of baptism mentioned in the New Testament is the *baptism of fire*. John the Baptist mentions this baptism in Luke 3:16. *John answered them all, "I baptize you with water. But one more powerful than I will come, the thongs of whose sandals I am not worthy to untie. He will baptize you with the Holy Spirit and with fire."*

We learned earlier that the baptism with water signifies repentance. Here we see that the coming of the Holy Spirit is proof of the presence of God. Fire is a biblical symbol of purification and power. John the Baptist said that Jesus will baptize us with the Holy Spirit and fire.

Let's talk about the baptism of fire first, specifically in the way it can purify us. Trials or difficult times that we go through are a type of baptism of fire. After John said Jesus would baptize us with the Holy Spirit and fire, he explains it more fully in the next verse. *His winnowing fork is in his hand to clear his threshing floor and to gather the wheat into his barn, but he will burn up the chaff with unquenchable fire (Luke 3:17).*

A fan or winnowing shovel was used to throw grain into the air so that the chaff would blow away, while the clean kernels fell back to the threshing floor. The Lord tells us that He will "clean out His threshing floor, and gather the wheat into His barn, and burn the chaff." In other words, our God is committed to cleaning out of our lives all of those unwholesome things (chaff) that may still be clinging to us. This could be habits from our past or old ways of thinking that are contrary to God's Word.

Baptism with fire
Isaiah 48:10; Philippians 1:29
2 Corinthians 5:7

This cleaning process is not always easy! Sometimes new Christians are shocked when they have to face trials in their lives. They assumed that the Christian life was going to be a life of ease.

I grew up on a farm, so I clearly understand the importance of the chaff being separated from the wheat in order to get a clean product. When wheat harvest came each year, we had a large vibrating screen that the wheat was poured onto which literally shook the chaff free as it was separated from the wheat. God is looking for good fruit (wheat) in our lives. Sometimes He allows us to be in circumstances to "vibrate" us a bit until the "chaff" in our lives can be blown away.

On the family farm, I also learned a similar lesson while welding. I remember taking a torch and heating metal until it was very hot. When it was hot, the impurities came to the top. We called it *slag*. When the slag surfaced, we would scrape it off, or it could keep the two pieces of metal from being properly welded together. Again, this is a picture of a separation of the good from the bad so that we can find purity.

There are times when we need the *slag* skimmed out of our lives in a baptism of fire. When we go through these fiery trials and hard times, the impurities will "come to the top" in our lives. The wrong attitudes, those things that irritate us, the critical spirit, lack of love, lack of joy, lack of patience,

REFLECTION
*What is some "chaff"
in your life that God is
cleaning away?*

attitude, behavior

fear—all "come to the top." When the "spiritual slag" is revealed in our lives, we can receive from Jesus the ability to repent and get rid of the impurities.

Drinking the cup

James and John, two of the disciples, had some *chaff* or *slag* in their lives that needed to be eradicated so they could become stronger. They sincerely loved Jesus and wanted to be close to Him, but they seemed to be focusing mainly on the benefits Jesus could give them when they sent their mother to ask a favor of Jesus on their behalf. When their mother asked if her sons could sit on the right and left side of Jesus in His kingdom, Jesus asked the following hard question, *"...Are you able to drink the cup that I am about to drink, and be baptized with the baptism that I am baptized with?" They said to Him, "We are able." So He said to them, "You will indeed drink My cup, and be baptized with the baptism that I am baptized with..." (Matthew 20:22-23 NKJ).*

Were they willing to be baptized with the baptism that He was to be baptized with—namely, to go to the cross? Were they willing to suffer in order to build the kingdom? Were they willing to face the impurities in their lives and allow Jesus to change them? They thought they were ready, so they said, "We are able." However, a few days later, they deserted their Master when He was arrested. The benefits of following Jesus just became less desirable to them when it involved suffering for Him!

Of course, the disciples later returned to Jesus after they had betrayed and abandoned Him. They witnessed His love and forgiveness in their lives. Jesus knows and understands our weaknesses. When the impurities come out of our lives, He reaches out with forgiveness and love. His power strengthens us so we can be victorious the next time we are faced with life's difficulties.

REFLECTION

Can you see how God is molding you through the baptism of fire to become the person He needs for the task He wants you to accomplish?

Yes - + it is hard.

Count it all joy

You may say, "Man, I'm having some hard times! Why me?" It is never easy when God allows us to go through the fire. It can make us feel like giving up when God doesn't make sense to us. What God really wants us to do is keep trusting Him. This is why James 1:2-5 tells us, *Consider it pure joy, my brothers, whenever you face trials of many kinds, because you know that the testing of your faith develops perseverance. Perseverance must finish its work so that you may be mature and complete, not lacking anything. If any of you lacks wisdom, he should ask God, who gives generously to all without finding fault, and it will be given to him.*

When we understand that the trials of life can be used by the Lord to work His character in our lives, it really changes our perspective. We can rejoice, because the Lord is using it for our good! And He promises to give us wisdom right in the middle of the trials if we just ask Him! He can be trusted, in spite of the pain.

I took a course in high school learning how to make certain metal tools. In order for the tools to be hardened, we were taught to take a hot molten piece of metal and dip it in and out of water in order to temper it. This process gave the tool the proper strength to be useful.

Our Lord allows us to go through the baptism of fire in order to make us useful in His service. An attitude of pride will not hold up under pressure. When we go through some fiery trials in life, we learn to trust in the Lord and in His Word. His character is built into our lives. Without His character built into our lives, we will break under pressure when the Lord really begins to use us.

REFLECTION
In what ways are you different after going through trials and tribulations? A little slower to react emotionally

DAY 6

Persevering in our trials

Yes, the Lord will use us, even when we are going through hard times! For example, did you ever have a brother or sister "sandpaper" in your life—someone who rubbed you the wrong way? Maybe the Lord allowed this person in your life for a reason. Perhaps He wanted to see if you would respond in a Christ-like way. So you reached out to the Lord for His strength to love this person unconditionally. It was not easy, and life was unpleasant for awhile, but you came through this baptism of fire with a new love and awareness of God's grace and mercy. Today you have a great relationship with this former "sister sandpaper"! Trusting Him and persevering really made you strong and cleaned out some bad attitudes in your own life.

Persevering in our trials
James 1:2-4
1 Corinthians 10:13
Romans 8:18,28

Did you ever pinch your finger causing a painful blood clot to form under the fingernail? You will probably have to go to the doctor so he can use a sterile needle to drill a little hole in the nail, releasing the pressure. The Lord wants us to release spiritual pressure in the lives of others. But, He can only use us effectively if our attitudes are pure and we trust Him.

When we persevere in our trials, we are purified by the Word of God so we can be the pure bride of Christ. The Bible calls the church "the bride of Christ." Did you ever see a dirty bride? I haven't. The Lord is cleaning us up. The book of Ephesians 5:25-27 says, *Husbands, love your wives, just as Christ loved the church and gave himself up for her to make her holy, cleansing her by the washing with water through the word, and to present her to himself as a radiant church, without stain or wrinkle or any other blemish, but holy and blameless.*

The Lord uses His Word to wash us. However, if we never look into the mirror, we tend to forget how dirty we can be. The Word of God is our mirror and our cleanser. As a little boy, I hated to take baths. But my parents made sure that I took a regular bath, whether I liked it or not! And now, I'm glad they did. You, too, will look back later and really appreciate your "spiritual bath."

REFLECTION
Have you seen spiritual growth in your life after coming through a trial? Yes
How did God's Word help you?
It helps take the focus off circumstances & puts it on Jesus.

Don't be afraid of the baptism of fire. Jesus will give you the strength to persevere. Trials can make you strong if you respond to them the right way.

On fire for Jesus

Previously we said that fire is a symbol of purification and power, and we have examined how we can be purified by "fiery" trials. Another side to the baptism of fire is the *power* aspect of it. We should live in such a way that our lives are "on fire for Jesus Christ." We need to be earnest and enthusiastic in our love for God, according to Revelation 3:19, and...*turn from your [our] indifference and become enthusiastic about the things of God (TLB).*

If we are not enthusiastic about the things of God, we are commanded to turn from our indifference or apathy. We have been created to experience His "fire" burning inside of us, baptized with fire. The early disciples "burned" with a zeal for God. Ask the Lord to baptize you with His fire and His zeal. God is looking for zealous men and women. Numbers 25:11-13 speaks of such a zealous man. *Phinehas son of Eleazar, the son of Aaron, the priest, has turned my anger away from the Israelites; for he was as zealous as I am for my honor among them, so that in my zeal I did not put an end to them. Therefore tell him I am making my covenant of peace with him. He and his descendants will have a covenant of a lasting priesthood, because he was zealous for the honor of his God and made atonement for the Israelites.* The Lord honored

REFLECTION

Are you enthused about what God is doing in your life? Are you full of zeal for Jesus?

Selfishly yes, as much as I should be No.

Phinehas because he was zealous for his God. Are you zealous for your God today? Are you experiencing this type of *baptism of fire*?

Those who are baptized with fire are men and women of prayer who have a holy hatred for sin, and a holy love for the Lord with a compassion for the lost and for the church of Jesus Christ. The psalmist in Psalms 69:9 reveals his righteous zeal for God's house and kingdom...*zeal for your house consumes me....* When we are truly on fire for God, all the desires of our body and soul are wrapped up in His desires. We are absorbed in who God wants us to be and what He wants us to do. We will have a godly zeal to see His house (His church) be all that it was created to be in our generation. "Lord, baptize us in your fire!"

Baptism in the Holy Spirit Part 1

KEY MEMORY VERSE
But you will receive power when the
Holy Spirit comes on you...
Acts 1:8

The promise of the Holy Spirit

So far in this book, we have covered three baptisms: baptism in water, baptism into the body of Christ, and baptism of fire. In this chapter and the next, we will look at the *baptism in the Holy Spirit.* It is important to realize how the Holy Spirit desires to use us and flow from our lives. The subject of the baptism in the Holy Spirit is sometimes a controversial one in today's Christian church, so let's carefully look at this experience to help us understand it better.

Let's look again at Luke 3:16. *John answered them all, "I baptize you with water. But one more powerful than I will come, the thongs of whose sandals I am not worthy to untie. He will baptize you with the Holy Spirit and with fire."* When we previously mentioned this verse, we covered the

The Holy Spirit has characteristics of God
Thinks: Romans 8:27; 1 Corinthians 2:10-11
Feels: Romans 15:30; Ephesians 4:30
Wills: 1 Corinthians 12:11
Has the capacity to enjoy our fellowship

baptism of fire part of it. Now we want to look at what John the Baptist meant when he said Jesus would baptize us *with the Holy Spirit.*

All genuine believers have the Spirit of God dwelling in them. I Corinthians 3:16 says, *Don't you know that you yourselves are God's temple and that God's Spirit lives in you?* The Holy Spirit lives within each child of God. The Holy Spirit is a person, not a doctrine or merely an influence or power. This is very important. The Holy Spirit is God and has the personal characteristics of God. God is the Father, Son, and Holy Spirit—

REFLECTION
Who is the Holy Spirit?

often referred to as the Trinity (see Biblical Foundation 7, Chapter 1, Day 2, for more on the Trinity). The Holy Spirit is the third person of the Trinity.

The divine person of the Holy Spirit comes to dwell in you when you give your life to Jesus and receive Him into your life. He cares about you and has the power to help you. However, this does not mean you have been *baptized* in the Holy Spirit.

The Holy Spirit lives within every believer

At the time of our salvation, the Holy Spirit comes to live within us. He leads and motivates us to live holy lives and delivers us from the bondage of sin. Romans 8:9 says, *You, however, are controlled not by the sinful nature but by the Spirit, if the Spirit of God lives in you. And if anyone does not have the Spirit of Christ, he does not belong to Christ.*

During Jesus' last talk with His disciples before His trial and crucifixion, He promised them they would receive the Holy Spirit (John 14:17). Subsequently, after His resurrection, Jesus visited the disciples and breathed on them saying...*Receive the Holy Spirit (John 20:22).*

At that moment, the disciples were born again by the Holy Spirit. Although the disciples had already confessed Jesus as Lord and were saved according to the old covenant provisions, they could not have been born again before Jesus was raised from the dead. Jesus had to come and give them His resurrection power according to the new covenant. Now they also believed that Jesus was raised from the dead, and their salvation was completed.

When God took a hunk of clay in the Garden of Eden and breathed on it, Adam was formed and received physical life. Here, God breathed on the disciples and gave them spiritual life. When you were convicted of your sin before you received Christ, the Holy Spirit was outside of you bringing conviction. When you received Jesus, the Holy Spirit then came *inside* to live within you. But there's more! The New Testament depicts *two* distinct yet complementary aspects of receiving the Holy Spirit—the experience of the disciples receiving the Holy Spirit on "Resurrection Sunday" that we just described, and the experience they later received on "Pentecost Sunday." Let's compare the two experiences in the next section.

REFLECTION
How can you be sure you have the Holy Spirit living in you? When do Christians receive the Holy Spirit?

You shall receive power!

After the disciples' encounter with the Holy Spirit when Jesus breathed on them and told them to "receive the Holy Spirit," He made it clear that their experience was still incomplete. In His final words to them before His ascension, He commanded them not to go out and preach immediately, but to go back to Jerusalem and wait there until they were baptized in the Holy Spirit and thus given the power they needed to be effective witnesses. *Do not leave Jerusalem, but wait for the gift my Father promised, which you have heard me speak about. For John baptized with water, but in a few days you will be baptized with the Holy Spirit...you will receive power when the Holy Spirit comes on you; and you will be my witnesses in Jerusalem, and in all Judea and Samaria, and to the ends of the earth (Acts 1:4-5,8).*

Baptism in the Holy Spirit
Luke 24:49-51
John 16:7-14, Acts 1:4

So the disciples prayed and waited. During the festival of Pentecost, 120 of His disciples were gathered together in one place, and it happened! *When the day of Pentecost came, they were all together in one place. Suddenly a sound like the blowing of a violent wind came from heaven and filled the whole house where they were sitting. They saw what seemed to be tongues of fire that separated and came to rest on each of them. All of them were filled with the Holy Spirit and began to speak in other tongues as the Spirit enabled them (Acts 2:1-4).*

Here, the disciples experienced the mighty baptism in the Holy Spirit. Although they had received the life of the Holy Spirit only a few weeks before when Jesus breathed on them (John 20:22), this time they received the *baptism* in the Holy Spirit. They received a new dimension of the Holy Spirit's power.

This distinction between receiving the Holy Spirit at rebirth and receiving the *baptism in the Holy Spirit* is significant. We need to recognize the difference between having the Holy Spirit living within us and being baptized in the Holy Spirit. The baptism in the Holy Spirit is the Lord's provision for releasing the power of the Holy Spirit into the believer's life.

The story is told of a Christian man who lived in a poor village in the interior of his nation who had the opportunity to come to a big city. Having never experienced the use of electricity before, he was fascinated when he saw electric light bulbs for the first time. He asked his host if he could have one to take back to his home. When he got back to his village, he hung the light bulb on a string in his hut. He was frustrated because it wouldn't work, until a missionary explained to him that it must be plugged into a power source. That's the way it is with us. To enter into the fullness of what God has planned for our lives, we have no greater need than to be plugged into the power source. We need the mighty baptism in the Holy Spirit. It is the gateway into a new dimension of the Spirit's presence and power in our lives, and it empowers us for ministry.

REFLECTION

Have you experienced the power of the Holy Spirit? Describe your experience.

We receive by faith

Just like salvation comes by faith, so the baptism in the Holy Spirit comes by faith. We receive the baptism in the Holy Spirit by faith in the Word of God and by faith in Jesus Christ. Faith is always a prerequisite for receiving the baptism in the Holy Spirit. Galatians 3:14 tells us explicitly...*that by faith we might receive the promise of the Spirit.*

Not everyone's experience will be the same. We can pray and receive the Holy Spirit baptism on our own or have someone pray for us to receive the power of the Spirit. Some believers have a dynamic, emotional experience at the time of their Holy Spirit baptism. They may begin to sing a new song that God gave to them in an unknown language or speak in tongues. Others simply take God at His Word and experience the reality of the baptism in the Holy Spirit as a process over the days and weeks that follow.

The type of experience that we have is not of primary importance; the key is that we know by faith in the Word of God that we've been filled and baptized with the Holy Spirit. We need to *know* we are baptized with the Spirit just as we need to *know* we have been born again.

It is possible to be baptized in water and in the Holy Spirit at the same time. Or, some may be baptized in the Holy Spirit before they are water-baptized. It happened in Acts 10:44-46. Peter was preaching the gospel to the Gentiles in Cornelius's home when an amazing phenomenon occurred. *While Peter was still speaking these words, the Holy Spirit came on all who heard the message. The circumcised believers who had come with Peter were astonished that the gift of the Holy Spirit had been poured out even on the Gentiles. For they heard them speaking in tongues and praising God.* The people at Cornelius' house received the Word and were saved. The Lord immediately poured out the Holy Spirit on them in power, thus paralleling the disciples' experience at Pentecost. The Holy Spirit baptism brings the personal boldness and power of the Spirit into our lives that we need to be effective.

REFLECTION
By what means do we receive the baptism in the Holy Spirit?

Regardless of our personal experience, the baptism in the Holy Spirit is received by faith. A pastor and his wife came to me and said, "We're not sure we've been baptized in the Holy Spirit." I assured them they can know for sure as I laid my hands on them and prayed. This time, they chose to "receive the promise of the Spirit through faith," and they were gloriously baptized with the Holy Spirit! From that time on, they knew it. Their spiritual thirst led them to yield to and receive the baptism in the Holy Spirit.

Want to be effective? It's your decision

Some might ask, "Do I really have to be baptized in the Holy Spirit?"

My reply would be, "Do you really need to have all of God's power so you can help other people find God?" People all around us are going to hell. We *need* God's power so He can fulfill His purpose in us and through us!

I often explain the power of the Holy Spirit like this. If you mow a lawn, you can do it with a scissors or with a lawn mower. It's your decision. You don't have to be baptized in the Holy Spirit to be a Christian, but like using the mower, God wants us to be effective. In fact, the early disciples of Jesus made being filled with the Holy Spirit a requirement for anyone who was to be set apart for special responsibilities in the church. *Brothers, choose seven men from among you who are known to be full of the Spirit and wisdom. We will turn this responsibility over to them (Acts 6:3).*

The baptism in the Holy Spirit increases the effectiveness of a Christian's witness because of a strengthening relationship with the

Father, Son and Holy Spirit that comes from being filled with the Spirit. The Holy Spirit makes the personal presence of Jesus more real to us, and it results in wanting to love and obey Him more.

A survey was taken in the Philippines some time back which found that each Christian who had received the baptism of the Holy Spirit brought 36 people to Christ compared to the 1 person led to the Lord by each Christian who had not received the Holy Spirit baptism. Why? The spirit-baptized Christians simply had the power of God in their lives to witness with greater effect.

REFLECTION

Describe a time you have experienced a greater effectiveness because of the baptism in the Holy Spirit.

You may say you know of Christians who are not baptized in the Holy Spirit. So do I. But think how much more effective they would be if they were baptized in the Spirit.

Saul's experiences with the Holy Spirit

Saul was a devout Jew who was playing havoc with the Christians in the book of Acts. He was on his way to Damascus to persecute the early Christians when the Lord met him and did something supernatural in his life. *"Who are you, Lord?" Saul asked. "I am Jesus, whom you are persecuting," he replied. "Now get up and go into the city, and you will be told what you must do." Then Ananias went to the house and entered it. Placing his hands on Saul, he said, "Brother Saul, the Lord—Jesus, who appeared to you on the road as you were coming here—has sent me so that you may see again and be filled with the Holy Spirit" (Acts 9:5,6,17).*

Ananias called Saul "brother" because Saul was now a Christian. However, Saul still wasn't filled with the Holy Spirit. Many people say that when you're saved, you are also automatically baptized in the Spirit. Although it is possible to receive and be baptized in the Holy Spirit at conversion, it is not always so. Saul, who became Paul, was baptized in the Holy Spirit three days after he received Christ into his life. It happened when Ananias laid his hands on Saul and prayed.

The difference between receiving the Holy Spirit at salvation and being baptized in the Holy Spirit can be explained like this: You can be led to a pool of water and drink from it (receive the Holy Spirit at salvation), or you can jump fully into the water (be baptized with the Holy Spirit). It's the same water (Holy Spirit) but you have a completely different experience.

During the late 1800's, evangelist Dwight L. Moody was preaching and saw the same two ladies sitting in the front row night after night. Nearly every night, they came up to him after his meetings and said, "Mr. Moody, you need to be filled with the Holy Spirit." At first he resisted their remarks. How-

REFLECTION
Explain the difference between receiving the Holy Spirit and being baptized in the Holy Spirit. Why do you think every person's experience is a bit different?

ever, months later, as he walked down a street in New York City, he had an experience with God and was filled with the Holy Spirit.

The results were amazing! He preached the same sermons, but instead of two or three people getting saved at his services, hundreds and thousands came to know Jesus. In his lifetime, a million people were kept out of hell because of the power of God on his life. What made the difference? The mighty baptism—infilling—of the Holy Spirit. He had received power.

Experiencing His power for yourself

I was baptized in the Holy Spirit seven years after I received Jesus Christ as my Lord. I could have been baptized in the Holy Spirit sooner, but I was ignorant of the Holy Spirit's work. Although I loved the Lord and was part of a youth ministry, I realized there was something missing in my life. I needed the power of the Holy Spirit. I sometimes attended Christian ministries where people were set free from drugs or other life-controlling problems, and I realized these people had a spiritual power that I didn't have.

After studying the scripture and being convinced this experience was based on the Word of God, I went out into the woods one day and prayed, "God, I want You to baptize me in the Holy Spirit." I prayed, but nothing happened. In retrospect, I can see that I had pride in my heart. I wanted to receive the baptism in the Holy Spirit alone, on my own terms. I didn't really want anything too radical to happen! So, I humbled myself and went to a pastor who laid hands on me and prayed for me. That night I received the baptism of the Holy Spirit.

After I was baptized in the Holy Spirit, my life immediately took on a whole new dimension of power. It wasn't me—it was God—the baptism in the Holy Spirit gave me an intense desire to please Him. Before I was baptized in the Holy Spirit, I was involved in a ministry where a few people had given their lives to the Lord. However, after I was baptized in the Holy Spirit, everything seemed to change. Hundreds of young people gave their lives to Christ during the next few years. I knew that it certainly wasn't anything that I was doing in my own power and strength. It was the Holy Spirit's power.

I must admit, that at first, I was not sure if I should share this experience with others because it was so controversial in the church at that time. I changed my mind when a young lady reprimanded me by saying, "Why didn't you tell me about the baptism in the Holy Spirit? Last Saturday night I was baptized with the Holy Spirit, and now I have experienced His power in my life." If you filled a kerosene lantern with oil, you would still have to strike a match and light the lantern so its power could be released. The same principle applies to the truth of the Holy Spirit. We can have the Holy Spirit living in us but lack the power He can release in our lives. God spoke to me through this young lady, and from that time on, I told people the truth I had discovered. It was a joy to serve as a "spiritual midwife" when Jesus baptized them in His precious Holy Spirit!

REFLECTION
The baptism in the Holy Spirit is for whom?

Although it took me *several* years from the time I was saved to the time I was baptized in the Holy Spirit, I believe it is God's will that we are born again and immediately receive the baptism in the Holy Spirit and the power of God in our lives. Acts 2:38-39 says the baptism in the Holy Spirit was not just for those at Pentecost, but for all who would believe in Christ throughout this age...*and you will receive the gift of the Holy Spirit. The promise is for you and your children and for all who are far off....*

CHAPTER 4

Baptism in the Holy Spirit Part 2

Receive God's good gift

Some sincere believers have told me they heard negative things about Spirit-baptized people. So have I. But, we live by the Word of God, not by other people's experiences. We may see something happen in the name of the Holy Spirit that may not be the Holy Spirit at all and think, "If that's the Holy Spirit, I want nothing to do with it." But we cannot throw out the baptism of the Holy Spirit because of what we saw or experienced that was not authentic.

Others may say, "If I'm supposed to be filled with the Holy Spirit, well, that's up to God...I'm open to whatever the Lord wants to do." This sounds like a noble response, but in reality, it may be a statement of unbelief because they do not really want to be filled. A young man told me once that he felt he did not deserve to be baptized with the Holy Spirit. I told him, "You're right. I don't deserve it either. We don't deserve salvation or anything else, but God wants to give it to us as a free gift."

God has already initiated His part in our receiving Christ and being baptized with the Holy Spirit. It's now up to us to receive by faith what He has freely offered. To be baptized with the Holy Spirit is a personal act of faith, a decision that we make. Our heavenly Father wants to give us the gift of the Holy Spirit. *If you then, though you are evil, know how to give good gifts to your children, how much more will your Father in heaven give the Holy Spirit to those who ask him! (Luke 11:13).*

Have you been baptized in the Holy Spirit? If you are not sure, ask! Jesus wants to baptize you with the Holy Spirit. You only need to ask Him in faith, in the same way that a child would ask his father for a gift.

Your heavenly Father wants you to receive the Holy Spirit, and He offers the baptism in the Holy Spirit to you freely! Suppose I gave you a Christmas gift and you took it home and opened it and found many gifts wrapped up inside. One of these gifts is a tool you needed, a pliers. But you must take the pliers out and use it in order for it to be effective. The same principle applies to the Spirit of God. We need to receive the gift of the baptism in the

REFLECTION

Gifts must be accepted, opened and used in order to really experience them. How do we accept the gift of tongues God offers to His children?

Holy Spirit by faith, and then begin to use all the wonderful individual spiritual gifts that accompany it.

What about tongues?

In Ephesus, some of the believers had never even heard of the Holy Spirit. So Paul instructed them, telling how they could receive the Holy Spirit. When he prayed for them, the Holy Spirit came upon them and they spoke with tongues. *When Paul placed his hands on them, the Holy Spirit came on them, and they spoke in tongues...(Acts 19:6).*

There are nine supernatural gifts of the Holy Spirit listed in 1 Corinthians 12:7-10. (For more about *using* these gifts, see Biblical Foundation Series book #4, Chapter 1, Day 4) The gift we want to look at in this chapter is the gift of tongues. *Now to each one the manifestation of the Spirit is given for the common good. To one there is given through the Spirit the message of wisdom, to another the message of knowledge by means of the same Spirit, to another faith by the same Spirit, to another gifts of healing by that one Spirit, to another miraculous powers, to another prophecy, to another distinguishing between spirits, to another speaking in different kinds of tongues, and to still another the interpretation of tongues.*

Often, when believers are baptized in the Holy Spirit, they begin to speak in *tongues* or a new heavenly language. The Bible says they magnify God (Acts 10:46). This personal prayer language is understood by God because it is my spirit speaking to God. Speaking in tongues is a direct line of communication between me and God.

In the book of Acts, speaking in tongues was often the initial outward sign accompanying the baptism in the Holy Spirit (Acts 2:4;10:45-46;19:6). Should every Spirit-filled believer speak with tongues, then? No, you don't have to, but you may! It's like going into a shoe store and getting a pair of shoes and saying, "Must I have tongues in my shoes?" No! But you take the tongues because they are part of the shoes! Praying in tongues is a blessing from God. Let's imagine that you came to my home and I gave you a meal. You say, "Must I eat this steak?" or "Must I eat this salad?" Well, no, you don't have to, but it is available for you as part of the whole meal deal!

God wants us to have and use spiritual gifts so that we may be a blessing to others. We need to exercise them so they can be used in our lives to build us up spiritually to give us supernatural strength and ability to be effective in our Christian lives. 1 Corinthians 14:1 says...*eagerly desire spiritual gifts....*

And Jude 20 tells us to...*build yourselves up in your most holy faith and pray in the Holy Spirit.*

REFLECTION
According to Acts 10:46, what is the purpose of tongues?

God wants us to build ourselves up in faith so we may be the powerful witnesses. In Acts 1:8 we read that when the Holy Spirit comes upon us, we will receive power to be His witnesses. That's why we receive power—to be His witnesses. Praying in tongues builds us up spiritually. It's like charging your spiritual battery. You can, with power, pray for the sick, and minister to people and help them as you continue to build up yourself spiritually by praying in other tongues.

I wish you all spoke in tongues

DAY 3

Speaking in tongues has been controversial in some parts of the church of Jesus Christ. One of the first times that I went to a public meeting where I was told that some of the people spoke in tongues, I sat near the back of the building. I wanted to make a quick exit if I became too uncomfortable! Although some believers hesitate because they have heard or seen misuses of the gift of tongues or other gifts of the Spirit, we have no need to be afraid.

It seems funny to recall now, but one of the fears that I had when I was considering being baptized in the Holy Spirit was that I would be in a place like a department store and the Spirit of God would come on me. I was afraid I'd begin to speak in tongues uncontrollably. I pictured myself being so embarrassed! Then one day I read this scripture, *The spirits of prophets are subject to the control of prophets (1 Corinthians 14:32).*

Your spirit is subject to you. It's like a water spigot. You turn it off and on. The water is always there, but it's under your control. You choose to pray or not to pray in tongues at any given time, but it's God who gives you the gift and the power to speak.

How important then is it for us as Christians to speak in tongues and exercise other spiritual gifts? Paul the apostle wished that every person spoke in tongues and stressed that the gift of tongues was an important part of his spiritual life. *I would like every one of you to speak in tongues...I thank God that I speak in tongues more than all of you (1 Corinthians 14:5a;14:18).*

Is someone a second-rate Christian if they don't speak in tongues? No, of course not! But God wants us to be blessed and use these blessings so we can fulfill His call on our lives.

REFLECTION

Why are some Christians afraid to receive the gift of tongues?

Some say they believe it is selfish to pray in tongues. Is it selfish to pray? Is it selfish to read the Bible? Why do we pray and read the scriptures and speak in tongues? We do it to communicate with God and in order to be built up spiritually so we can be effective in helping other people.

Bypassing the devil!

We pray two ways—with our mind and with our spirit. Both are needed, and both are under the influence of the Holy Spirit, according to 1 Corinthians 14:14-15. *For if I pray in a tongue, my spirit prays, but my mind is unfruitful. So what shall I do? I will pray with my spirit, but I will also pray with my mind; I will sing with my spirit, but I will also sing with my mind.*

The first way we pray is with our mind. When we pray, "Our Father in heaven..." it's coming from our mind. We understand it. We are using our intellect to pray in a learned language.

The second way we pray is with our spirit. When we pray with our spirit (in tongues), it's unfruitful to our mind. Our spirit is praying directly to the Father without having to accept the limitations of our human intellect.

In other words, when you and I pray with our spirit, we have no idea what we are saying, but our heavenly Father knows what we're saying. We come in simple faith and trust God to provide the form of the words and their meaning to Him. Using our new language, we edify ourselves (1 Corinthians 14:4) or "build ourselves up" spiritually. It is like a direct phone line to God.

I walked into a hardware store one night soon after I was baptized in the Holy Spirit and there were two men conversing in "Pennsylvania Dutch," a language many people of German descent use in my community. I cannot understand this language at all. Even though I didn't understand, those men understood one another clearly. The Spirit of God spoke to me and said, "In the same way that these two men understand one another, I understand exactly what you are saying when you pray in tongues. Continue to praise Me and magnify Me in this new language I've given to you." I was set free to pray in tongues from that day on without the nagging thoughts of unbelief and doubt from the devil.

Today, I pray in tongues daily, because when I pray in tongues, I bypass the devil. He has no idea what I'm saying. I'm speaking the "language of angels" and "mysteries" according to God's Word...*I speak with the tongues of men and of angels...(1 Corinthians 13:1).*

REFLECTION
*How can the gift of tongues help me to pray?
Do I know what I am saying when I pray in tongues?
Does the devil know what I am saying?*

For anyone who speaks in a tongue does not speak to men but to God. Indeed, no one understands him; he utters mysteries with his spirit (1 Corinthians 14:2).

Kinds of tongues

To clarify some common misconceptions of tongues, let's look at two different kinds of tongues mentioned in God's Word. The kind of tongues we have mentioned so far is for personal prayer and intercession. This is the type of tongues that magnifies God and is a direct line of communication between us and God. It is God speaking through us. *In the same way, the Spirit helps us in our weakness. We do not know what we ought to pray for, but the Spirit himself intercedes for us with groans that words cannot express. And he who searches our hearts knows the mind of the Spirit, because the Spirit intercedes for the saints in accordance with God's will (Romans 8:26-27).*

P. C. Nelson, founder of the Southwestern Bible Institute, was a Greek scholar. He told his young ministers that the Greek literally reads, "The Holy Spirit maketh intercession for us with groanings which cannot be uttered in articulate speech" (articulate speech is the ordinary kind of speech). He pointed out that the Greek bears out that this not only includes "groanings" in prayer, but also "other tongues." [1] The Bible tells us that the Holy Spirit helps us to pray. Many times I have felt unable to put into words the desires of my heart when I pray. And sometimes, situations are so complex that I just do not know how to pray. But the Holy Spirit does!

The second type of tongues is mentioned in 1 Corinthians 12:28-30 after God says He has appointed some in the church for various tasks and responsibilities. *And in the church God has appointed first of all apostles, second prophets, third teachers, then workers of miracles, also those having gifts of healing, those able to help others, those with gifts of administration, and those speaking in different kinds of tongues. Are all apostles? Are all prophets? Are all teachers? Do all work miracles? Do all have gifts of healing? Do all speak in tongues? Do all interpret?*

Because this scripture states, "Do all speak in tongues?" many think this means that not all can speak in tongues as a personal prayer language. However, this scripture is really asking, "Are all appointed to speak with the gift of tongues *to the church*?"

You see, there is a gift to be used *in the church* which is a type of speaking in tongues. It is different from the type of speaking in tongues that we experience when we pray in our prayer language. When this gift of tongues is used in the church, someone who has the gift gives a message in tongues, and someone with the *gift of interpretation* gives the meaning, thus building up the body of Christ.

To summarize, although all Christians may speak in tongues so we can be built up spiritually to serve God better, He also sometimes gives a special gift of tongues to be used to build up His church. These scriptures are clear that not all will be used by God to speak in tongues in a church meeting. However, we can still pray in tongues as a personal prayer language to the Lord. The same goes for the other gifts listed here. You and I may not have the gift of administration in the church, but we all must administer our checkbooks. We may not have the gift of healing, but we are all called to pray for the sick in our own families.

REFLECTION

Can you have and use your prayer tongue even if you do not use it publicly?

What is the purpose of tongues when the church meets together?

[1]*Seven Vital Steps To Receiving the Holy Spirit* by Kenneth E. Hagin, p. 10.

Eagerly desire

DAY 6

After Paul lists the ministry gifts of the Holy Spirit to the church, in 1 Corinthians 12:28-30, he says in verse 31, *But eagerly desire the greater gifts. And now I will show you the most excellent way.*

What is the greater gift? The greater gift depends on the situation you're in. If you need healing, you believe God for the "greater" gift of healing because that is what you need.

What is the "most excellent way?" It is love. 1 Corinthians, chapter 13, tells us all about it! Some say they don't need all these gifts; they just need love. That's not what Paul was trying to communicate. He is emphasizing that to possess spiritual gifts without love amounts to nothing. We need to use these gifts in love according to 1 Corinthians 13:8-13. *Love never fails. But where there are...tongues, they will be stilled...For we know in part and we prophesy in part, but when perfection comes, the imperfect disappears. When I was a child, I talked like a child, I thought like a child, I reasoned like a child. When I became a man, I put childish ways behind me. Now we see but a poor reflection as in a mirror; then we shall see face to face. Now I know in part; then I shall know fully, even as I am fully known. And now these three remain: faith, hope and love. But the greatest of these is love.*

REFLECTION
What is the best gift?
What is the more excellent way?

This passage of scripture reveals that tongues will cease when "that which is perfect is come." Some people believe that this means tongues are no longer needed today. They believe that "that which is perfect" refers to the Bible. However, they fail to realize that the same passage says we shall see "face to face." We will not see the Bible face to face. We will see Jesus face to face. At that time, at the end of the age, there will be no need for the gift of tongues. But until we see Jesus face to face, the Lord has given us the gifts of tongues and prophecy and other supernatural gifts of the Holy Spirit to use for His glory here on earth.

Continue to be filled with the Spirit

Do you know for sure that you are baptized with the Holy Spirit? Do you pray in tongues? Are the spiritual gifts becoming evident in your life? If you are not sure, ask Jesus to fill you with His precious Holy Spirit today. Ask another Spirit-filled believer to pray for you. Sometimes it takes someone else to agree with us in faith to experience the Holy Spirit's filling. Paul went to Ananias. The Samaritans waited for Peter and John. I went to a pastor friend.

We must reach out and receive the promise of the Spirit by faith. By faith we receive, and then are continually filled, day by day! Dwight L. Moody, the famous evangelist, used to say, "I need to be filled with the Holy Spirit every day, because I leak!"

The early believers knew this, too, according to Acts 4:31. *After they prayed, the place where they were meeting was shaken. And they were all filled with the Holy Spirit and spoke the word of God boldly.* Many of these believers were already filled with the Holy Spirit at Pentecost in Acts chapter 2. But they needed to be filled again. We, too, must experience constant renewal. Paul warns the believers that to maintain the fullness of the Spirit, they must live lives separate from sin. *Do not get drunk on wine, which leads to debauchery. Instead, be filled with the Spirit (Ephesians 5:18).*

The New Testament baptism in the Holy Spirit happens in the context of committed discipleship to Jesus Christ. Our hearts must be right with God so He can pour out His Spirit on us. As we live in obedience to Christ, there will be a greater awareness and presence of the Holy Spirit in our lives. We will deepen our relationship with the Father and grow in our love for others.

God wants to use you to see change come into people's lives.

REFLECTION
Why did the believers in Acts 4:31 have to be filled with the Holy Spirit again? Is there evidence of power in your life that you have been baptized in the Holy Spirit?

But it takes the Holy Spirit's power to "break through." The Lord wants to use you to touch others' lives for eternity. People in your family will be changed when you are baptized in the Holy Spirit. It may not happen immediately, but it will happen! It won't be through your natural ability, but by Christ who is at work in you through the Holy Spirit. God bless you as you live by the power and the authority of God and experience the Holy Spirit flowing through your life.

Baptism in Water

1. An elementary principle: Doctrine of baptisms
Hebrews 6:2

a. This foundational doctrine is plural: **doctrine of baptisms.**

b. We will look at four kinds of baptisms: baptism in water, baptism into the body of Christ, baptism of fire, and baptism in the Holy Spirit.

2. Baptism in water is a demonstration of obedience

a. Baptism is an outward sign of an inward cleansing from sin. It is an act of faith and obedience.

b. Jesus set the example (Matthew 3:15).

c. Baptism followed belief in Jesus (Mark 16:16).

d. Infant baptism not mentioned in the Bible.

3. Baptism in water makes a public announcement

a. First step of obedience is water baptism (Acts 2:38).

b. Makes a public announcement (Mark 1:4).

c. Christians are empowered to fulfill the Great Commission as they make disciples and baptize them.
Matthew 28:19-20

4. Baptism in water shows we are dead to sin and alive to Christ

a. Dead to sin, alive to Christ (Romans 6:4).

b. Water baptism is a sign of being buried to sin and resurrected to new life.

c. Our old life is dead.

Ex: Gangster Joe gave his life to Jesus. No longer the same.

d. Baptized in Greek means "to immerse." However, the mode is not as important as knowing your old nature is dead and you are now alive to Christ.

5. Baptism in water illustrates a New Testament circumcision

a. A type of New Testament circumcision.
Colossians 2:11-12

b. In Old Testament, a boy's foreskin was cut away as a sign of God's covenant to His people. Water baptism shows our sin nature has been cut away.

c. Bondage of the past is broken after coming through the water, just like children of Israel coming through Red Sea after bondage to Egypt (1 Corinthians 10:1-2).

d. Sin is not our master (Romans 6:14), our old self is crucified with Christ (Romans 6:6).

6. Baptism in water shows we are obeying God

a. We are exhorted to believe and be baptized (Mark 16:16).

b. Symbolizes a spiritual cleansing (1 Peter 3:21).

c. What about a deathbed conversion? (Luke 23:40-43).

d. Baptism shortly after conversion is the norm.
Acts 16:33; Acts 8:38; Acts 18:8

7. Be baptized in water!

a. What are you waiting for? Doubts can cloud your faith.
Romans 14:23

b. You do not need to be a pastor to baptize another. Paul trained others in the church to help him.
1 Corinthians 1:14,17

More Baptisms

1. Baptism into the body of Christ
1 Corinthians 12:13

a. Holy Spirit supernaturally places us into the body or family of God.

b. We are on earth to become Christ's hands, feet, tongue, etc. with various functions, gifts and callings.

2. God's wonderful family

a. When we are born again into God's family, we become brothers and sisters in Christ to every other believer in the world!

Ex: Visit to largest church in the world in Korea, met believers who spoke another language, but we were one!

b. God's family is made up of people from every nationality, race and culture (Revelation 5:9).

c. We are sons and daughters of the King of the Universe.
2 Corinthians 6:18

3. Baptism of fire
Luke 3:16

a. Fire is symbol of purification and power.

b. Trials or difficult times are a type of baptism of fire.

c. The Lord wants to purify us during these times (Luke 3:17), but the cleaning process may not be easy.

Ex: Separating the chaff from the wheat on a farm: involves shaking!

Welding: Involves skimming off the slag so two metals will adhere.

d. When spiritual *slag* is revealed in our lives, Jesus will help us get rid of those impurities.

4. Drinking the cup

   a. Jesus asked His disciples if they were willing to suffer for the cause of the kingdom (Matthew 20:22-23).

   b. Disciples said they were willing to suffer, but later deserted Jesus when He was arrested.

   c. Jesus reaches out with forgiveness because He understands our weakness. When impurities come out of our lives, He reaches out in love so we can be victorious.

5. Count it all joy

   a. God wants us to trust Him when we go through the fire. James 1:2-5

   b. His character is being worked into our lives and we become more useful in His service.

      Ex: For metal to be hardened, the molten piece of metal must be dipped in and out of water to temper it.

6. Persevering in our trials

   a. Brother or sister sandpaper who rubs you the wrong way. How will you respond?

      Ex: A painful blood clot under fingernail needs pressure released. The Lord will use us to release spiritual pressure on others' lives if our attitudes are pure.

   b. When we persevere in trials, we are purified by the Word of God (Ephesians 5:25-27).

7. On fire for Jesus

   a. Another side to the baptism of fire is the *power* aspect.

   b. We should be on fire for Jesus (Revelation 3:19).

   c. Early disciples burned with a zeal for God. Phinehas in the Old Testament, was honored by the Lord because he was zealous (Numbers 25:11-13).

   d. Are our desires wrapped up in His desires? (Psalms 69:9).

Baptism in the Holy Spirit
Part 1

1. The promise of the Holy Spirit

a. Jesus baptizes in the Holy Spirit (Luke 3:16).

b. All believers have the Holy Spirit dwelling in them.
1 Corinthians 3:16

c. Holy Spirit is a person—the third person of the Trinity.

2. The Holy Spirit lives within every believer

a. He motives us to live holy lives (Romans 8:9).

b. Before His crucifixion, Jesus promised disciples would receive the Holy Spirit (John 14:17).

c. After His resurrection, He breathed on them to receive the Holy Spirit (John 20:22). Disciples were then born again according to the new covenant.

3. You shall receive power!

a. After Jesus breathed on His disciples to *receive* the Holy Spirit, He made it clear their experience was incomplete.

b. Jesus told them to wait until they were *baptized* in the Holy Spirit, thus giving them power to witness (Acts 1:4-5,8).
Ex: A light bulb has no power without electricity.

4. We receive by faith

a. We receive the Holy Spirit by faith (Galatians 3:14).

b. The type of experience is not as important as knowing *by faith* we have been filled and baptized.

> *Ex: Not everyone's experience will be the same (Acts 10:44-46 believers were baptized in Holy Spirit before water baptism).*

5. Want to be effective? It's your decision

a. God wants us to be filled with the power of the Holy Spirit to be more effective.

b. It was required for those set apart in the early church.
Acts 6:3

> *Ex: Survey in Philippines: Spirit-filled believers brought more souls to Christ because they had power of God to witness with greater effect.*

6. Saul's second experience with the Holy Spirit

a. Saul was supernaturally saved and then waited until Ananias came to lay hands on him to receive the Holy Spirit's power. Acts 9:5,6,17

> *Ex: You can be led to pool of water and drink from it or jump into it!*

b. D.L. Moody's preaching had radical results after he was baptized in the Holy Spirit.

7. Experiencing His power for yourself

> *Ex: Personal testimony of Holy Spirit baptism.*

a. Baptism in Holy Spirit not just for those at Pentecost. Acts 2:38-39

b. Like a kerosene lantern with oil, which needs a match struck to light it, we need the baptism in the Holy Spirit ignited in us to release His power.

Baptism in the Holy Spirit
Part 2

1. Receive God's good gift

a. To be baptized in the Holy Spirit is a personal act of faith.

b. Baptism in the Holy Spirit is a gift (Luke 11:13). Ask!

   Ex: You have to open a gift and use it for it to be effective.

2. What about tongues?

a. Early Christians receive Holy Spirit and speak in tongues. Acts 19:6

b. The gift of tongues (1 Corinthians 12:7-10) is a heavenly language which magnifies God (Acts 10:46).

c. Tongues is often an outward sign of the baptism in the Holy Spirit (Acts 2:4;10:45-46;19:6).

d. Should eagerly desire spiritual gifts (1 Corinthians 14:1) so we can be built up spiritually.

3. I wish you all spoke in tongues

a. Speaking in tongues is not some out-of-control impulse! 1 Corinthians 14:32

b. Paul wished everyone spoke in tongues (1 Corinthians 14:5a; 14:18) because it was an important part of his spiritual life.

4. Bypassing the devil!

a. We pray with our mind and with our spirit. 1 Corinthians 14:14-15

b. We understand when we pray with our mind. When we pray with our spirit, we are praying directly to the Father without having to accept the limitations of our human intellect.

c. The devil cannot understand this language of angels. 1 Corinthians 13:1; 14:2

5. Kinds of tongues

a. Tongues for personal prayer and intercession.

Romans 8:26-27

When we do not know how to pray, Holy Spirit prays for us.

b. Gift of tongues to be used in the church:

1 Corinthians 12:28-30

The message in tongues is given and then interpreted in a known language.

6. Eagerly desire

a. When Paul lists the ministry gifts of the Holy Spirit to the church, he says we should eagerly desire the "greater gift" and a "more excellent way" (1 Corinthians 12:28-30).

b. The greater gift is what you need at the time: healing, etc. The excellent way is love.

c. To possess the gifts without love amounts to nothing.

d. Until we see Jesus face to face, the gifts, including tongues, are given to us to use for His glory on earth.

1 Corinthians 13:8-13

7. Continue to be filled with the Spirit

a. If you are not sure you are, ask to be baptized in the Holy Spirit today!

b. After we receive, we must continue to be filled because we leak!

c. Early believers were filled again (Acts 4:31) after they were filled at Pentecost (Acts 2).

d. To maintain the fullness of the Spirit, we must live lives separate from sin (Ephesians 5:18).

e. The baptism in the Holy Spirit happens in the context of committed discipleship to Jesus Christ.

Chapter 1
Baptism in Water
Journaling space for reflection questions

DAY 1

Name the four types of baptisms mentioned in the Bible. Think about how many of the four you have experienced.

DAY 2

If you have been water-baptized, recall your experience.

DAY 3

If you have been water-baptized, what does it mean to you, to Jesus, to your friends?

DAY 4 *What is the spiritual explanation of going under and coming back up out of the water? Can you truly say that your "old self" is dead?*

DAY 5 *As we pass through the water, we are symbolizing our freedom from our past bondage to _____(fill in the blank). Why is it important not to rely on our feelings?*

DAY 6 *What brings a clear conscience toward God?*

DAY 7 *If you have doubts about your conversion and baptism, what can you do about it?*

Chapter 2
More Baptisms
Journaling space for reflection questions

Who baptizes you into the body of Christ?

Think about a time you experienced kinship with a believer from a different culture. What did you have in common? truth?

What is some "chaff" in your life that God is cleaning away?

DAY 4 *Can you see how God is molding you through the baptism of fire to become the person He needs for the task He wants you to accomplish?*

DAY 5 *In what ways are you different after going through trials and tribulations?*

DAY 6 *Have you seen spiritual growth in your life after coming through a trial? How did God's Word help you?*

DAY 7 *Are you enthused about what God is doing in your life? Are you full of zeal for Jesus?*

Chapter 3
Baptism in the Holy Spirit
Part 1
Journaling space for reflection questions

DAY 1

Who is the Holy Spirit?

DAY 2

How can you be sure you have the Holy Spirit living in you?
When do Christians receive the Holy Spirit?

DAY 3

Have you experienced the power of the Holy Spirit?
Describe your experience.

By what means do we receive the baptism in the Holy Spirit?

Describe a time you have experienced a greater effectiveness because of the baptism in the Holy Spirit.

Explain the difference between receiving the Holy Spirit and being baptized in the Holy Spirit. Why do you think every person's experience is a bit different?

The baptism in the Holy Spirit is for whom?

Chapter 4
Baptism in the Holy Spirit
Part 2
Journaling space for reflection questions

DAY 1

Gifts must be accepted, opened and used in order to really experience them. How do we accept the gift of tongues God offers to His children?

DAY 2

According to Acts 10:46, what is the purpose of tongues?

DAY 3

Why are some Christians afraid to receive the gift of tongues?

How can the gift of tongues help me to pray? Do I know what I am saying when I pray in tongues? Does the devil know what I am saying?

Can you have and use your prayer tongue even if you do not use it publicly? What is the purpose of tongues when the church meets together?

What is the best gift? What is the more excellent way?

Why did the believers in Acts 4:31 have to be filled with the Holy Spirit again? Is there evidence of power in your life that you have been baptized in the Holy Spirit?

Daily Devotional Extra Days

If you are using this book as a daily devotional, you will notice there are 28 days in this study. Depending on the month, you may need the three extra days' studies given here.

DAY 29 | The Spirit of Truth?

Read John 16:13-14. These verses tell us of the work the Holy Spirit does in our lives. List them. What is the main work of the Holy Spirit? Who does the Holy Spirit hear speaking?
To whom does the Holy Spirit tell these truths?
Does the Holy Spirit ever speak to you? How can you know it is He?

DAY 30 | Rivers of Living Water

Read John 7:38-39. Here Jesus promises that believers would receive the Holy Spirit and He would flow out of their hearts like great rivers of life-giving water. What is life-giving water?
Toward whom does it flow? When was Jesus glorified?
Why was the Holy Spirit only given after this?

DAY 31 | Joy and the Holy Spirit

Read Acts 13:48-52. Are you a disciple of Christ? Explain. As we follow in the footsteps of the early disciples, what can we expect to experience? Are you experiencing persecution or trials?
Are you experiencing being filled with joy and the Holy Spirit? Explain.

Coordinates with this series!

Biblical Foundations for Children

Creative learning experiences for ages 4-12, patterned after the *Biblical Foundation Series*, with truths in each lesson. Takes kids on the first steps in their Christian walk by teaching them how to build solid foundations in their young lives. by Jane Nicholas, 176 pages: $17.95
ISBN:1-886973-35-0

Other books by Larry Kreider

House to House

The church is waking up to the simple, successful house to house strategy practiced by the New Testament church. *House to House* documents how God called a small fellowship of believers to become a house to house movement. During the past years, DOVE Christian Fellowship Int'l has grown into a family of cell-based churches and house churches networking throughout the world. by Larry Kreider, 206 pages: $8.95   ISBN: 1-880828-81-2

The Cry for Spiritual Fathers & Mothers

Returning to the biblical truth of spiritual parenting so believers are not left fatherless and disconnected. How loving, seasoned spiritual fathers and mothers help spiritual children reach their full potential in Christ. by Larry Kreider, 186 pages: $11.95 ISBN: 1-886973-42-3

The Biblical Role of Elders for Today's Church

New Testament leadership principles for equipping elders. What elders' qualifications and responsibilities are, how they are chosen, how elders are called to be armor bearers, spiritual fathers and mothers, resolving conflicts, and more. *by Larry Kreider, Ron Myer, Steve Prokopchak, and Brian Sauder.* $12.99 ISBN: 1-886973-62-8

Check our Web site: www.dcfi.org

Hearing God 30 Different Ways Seminar

Learn to "tune in" to God and discern "HIS" voice. God wants to speak to you. Each attendee receives a seminar manual.

Spiritual Fathering & Mothering Seminar

Practical preparation for believers who want to have and become spiritual parents. Each attendee receives a seminar manual.

Elder's and Church Leadership Training

Based on New Testament leadership principles, this seminar equips leaders to provide protection, direction and correction in the local church. Each attendee receives a seminar manual.

Small Groups 101 Seminar

Basics for healthy cell ministry. Session topics cover the essentials for growing cell group ministry. Each attendee receives a *Helping You Build Manual*.

Small Groups 201 Seminar

Takes you beyond the basics and into an advanced strategy for cell ministry. Each attendee receives a seminar manual.

Counseling Basics

This seminar takes you through the basics of counseling, specifically in small group ministry. Includes a comprehensive manual.

Marriage Mentoring Training Seminar

Trains church leaders and mature believers to help prepare engaged couples for a strong marriage foundation by using the mentoring format of *Called Together*. Includes a *Called Together Manual*.

**For additional seminars
and more information
www.dcfi.org
Call 800.848.5892
email: info@dcfi.org**